THE NEW
INVESTOR'S GUIDE TO
MAKING MONEY IN
RESIDENTIAL REAL ESTATE

About the authors

Jan Somers retired from teaching high school mathematics ten years ago to raise her family of three children, taking advantage of her time at home to further develop her interest in property investment. This was so successful that the family now have total financial security and a portfolio well in excess of a million dollars.

Dolf de Roos began investing in residential real estate while still an undergraduate student. Although he owns and manages an international technology company, most of his time is spent investing in real estate. Dr de Roos also conducts seminars on residential and commercial property investment, and his columns are syndicated in publications throughout the country.

THE NEW ZEALAND INVESTOR'S GUIDE TO MAKING MONEY IN RESIDENTIAL REAL ESTATE

by

Jan Somers and Dolf de Roos

SOMERSET FINANCIAL SERVICES
DE ROOS ASSOCIATES

*"Man's mind, once stretched by a new idea,
never regains its original dimensions."*

The laws relating to property investment are complex and constantly changing. Every effort has been made to ensure that this book is free from errors. No responsibility can be accepted by either the authors or printer for any action taken by any persons or organisations which relates to material in this book. All persons should satisfy themselves independently as to the relevancy of the material to their own particular situation.

Copies of this book are available from de Roos Associates, P.O. Box 14, Christchurch, New Zealand, at $27.50 including postage and packaging. See order form at back of book for details.

ISBN 0-473-01569-2

Printing history
First printing : March 1992
Second printing : June 1992
Third printing : December 1993
Fourth printing : July 1994
Fifth printing : March 1995
Sixth printing : June 1995
Seventh printing : October 1995
Eighth printing : February 1996
Ninth printing : April 1996
Tenth printing : October 1997

Typeset by CREATIVE IMAGING Ltd
Printed by TEAMPRINT Ltd
Christchurch, New Zealand

Introduction to the Tenth Printing

The first edition of this book was released in July 1992. Within three months, Infometrics published a report which boldly stated: "New Zealanders owning homes as investments will be better off in 20 years time if they sell their properties now and put the money in the bank". This report received front page attention in just about every newspaper in New Zealand, in stark contrast to my press release the following day which pointed out why the Infometrics predictions were patently absurd.

The government had just legislated that inflation be capped at 2%. With inflation capped at 2%, so the argument went, surely properties could not possibly rise at a higher rate? Well, a brief look at other countries (such as Germany) which have not only had periods of low inflation but also of deflation, would reveal that an artificial limit on inflation of itself has little or no influence on growth in property values. Such has also been the case in New Zealand, where despite the supposed 2% maximum inflation, values in parts of Auckland have more than doubled in recent years.

Of course the jury is still out on what will have happened after 20 years, but now, five years after the infamous Infometrics report, it is obvious that anyone who took the advice to heart, sold up, and put his money in the bank would now be licking his financial wounds. Median prices have moved from around $115,000 to over $150,000, which is substantial in itself, but when coupled with the generous taxation advantages and easy leverage which property affords, it means that over the last 5 years property has continued to be the superlative investment vehicle that it has been for generations.

This 10th edition has been updated so that the working examples reflect the new (as of July 1st 1996) taxation rates of 21.5% up to $34,200 and 33% thereafter (previously these were 24% up to $30,875 and 33% thereafter). Overall, however, the effect of these changes on property investors, while beneficial, will be minor. Indeed, one of the great delights of the property market is that the rules hardly change at all, which helps explain the ongoing popularity of this book as an introduction to the property market.

By the way, Infometrics rescinded its negative stance on property within months of releasing its headline grabbing report, claiming that "market conditions have changed". Interestingly enough, this change of heart was not headline news.

Dolf de Roos, October 1997

Introduction to the Fourth Printing

In the two and a half years since the first edition, there have been various changes to the property investment climate, most of which have been beneficial to the investor. Mortgage interest rates have come down from around 12%–14% to around 7.5%–9%; capital growth, which had slowed right down in some regions, is starting to pick up again; and property has once more become popular, as evidenced by the surge in demand resulting in the present sellers' market.

At my property seminars I always pointed out how generous the government depreciation allowances were on buildings – 2.5% for wooden buildings, 2% for brick, and 1% for steel-reinforced concrete. It is clear why the government allows us to depreciate cars or computers, as they do indeed go down in value over time, but surely the government is not so silly as to think that buildings go down in value? Why then would they allow us to depreciate buildings? I would point out that this was the government's way of encouraging us to invest in property so that we would help solve the housing problem. Inevitably someone at the seminar would claim that the depreciation allowances were a loop-hole, and that the government would change the law as soon as it realised its mistake.

As it turned out, the government *did* change the law: depreciation on all buildings purchased after April 1st 1993 was **increased** to 3% straight line or a massive 4% diminishing value (see section 4.1). Similarly, chattel depreciation allowances have increased dramatically (for example, the rate for carpets has increased from 20% to 33% diminishing value). The message is clear: the government does not consider itself an efficient provider of accommodation, and is encouraging us to do the task for them through such incentives as generous depreciation allowances and other tax write-offs.

Those people who bought property two years ago (let alone earlier) are generally doing extremely well. In the long run it doesn't matter whether we are presently in a buyer's market or seller's market, whether interest rates are going up or coming down, or whether the economic forecasters are telling us to buy or sell our houses. History shows us that over time property is an excellent investment. The implications (if not guarantees) for the future are obvious.

Dolf de Roos, July 1994

The New Zealand Investor's Guide to Making Money in Residential Real Estate

Table of Contents

Section 1. Introduction

About this book

The aim of this book is to show you how to achieve financial security by **investing long-term in income-producing residential property**. The strategy that we describe places emphasis on diverting short-term income into long-term asset building so that when your working life stops, your income doesn't. It neither pretends to be a "get-rich-quick" scheme, nor are the principles that it follows new. Nevertheless, it is our firm view that this approach offers one of the surest pathways to creating personal wealth; **this book attempts to provide a recipe for a personal "superannuation scheme" that has far better returns and much greater flexibility that the more recognised forms of superannuation.**

Why then haven't more people discovered property investment? Unfortunately, our education system does not teach people how best to manage their own financial affairs. Emphasis is placed on the teaching of skills to enable people to earn money but no time at all is devoted to the teaching of investment skills which result in long-term financial security. Although there are many investment products available today, direct property investment receives very little attention, possibly because the advice of many financial advisers is more aligned to the commissions they receive (and for direct property investment, this is nil). Another reason is that most people are not aware that they can actually afford to directly invest in property because they think they need about $100,000 before they can start. However, it can be shown that in many cases it may take as little as $80 per week to enter the property investment market.

But where can you go for help? Independent advice is often sought from bank managers, accountants and solicitors, whose expertise in property investment may be limited. Ask yourself this question. If you wanted to be the best cricketer, who would you ask for advice – the promoter (who handles the money), the scorekeeper (who does the sums and keeps the score), the umpire (who ensures that the rules are adhered to), or Sir Richard Hadlee (the player who has plenty of experience)? Clearly, if you want to be a successful property investor, you don't simply ask the advice of the bank manager (who handles the money), or the accountant (who does the sums and keeps the score), or the solicitor (who ensures that the rules are adhered to); rather you should seek the advice of experienced successful property investors (the experienced players). Bank managers, accountants and solicitors provide expert professional services in the areas in which they are qualified – not necessarily property investment.

This book is the culmination of 20 years of research and experience in property investment and outlines the philosophy and strategy used by us and many other successful investors in residential property. As well as this, the book provides the intricate detail associated with property selection (Section 2), finance (Section 3), taxation (Section 4), return on investment (Section 5), and property management (Section 6). Section 7 provides an "A to Z of What If" which gives answers to the most commonly asked questions, and Section 8 provides an annotated list for further reading on the subject.

The philosophy

The central theme of this book is to show you how to accumulate income producing residential property to keep long-term. You will be effectively creating your own personal superannuation, pension and insurance fund combined, but with returns that, in our experience and that of many others, outperform all other investments over the long-term.

The concept of "buying to keep" is difficult for many people to accept because they consider that the only way to make a profit is to buy and sell. You do not have to sell to make a profit. By keeping the property you can actually re-invest in further property and put your profit back to work. It is often the case that many so-called "investors", having sold property to realise their profits, sit on the money for several months before deciding that property really was the best option and subsequently re-invest in property. This little exercise of buying and selling may cost as much as $10,000. Too many investors enter the market with a short-term view that is reinforced by a "myopic media" who sell papers by reporting a myriad of short-term crises. High interest rates, fuel shortages, down-turns in the economy and recessions rarely affect long-term property investment. Evidence of this is the fact that for the last 900 years in Great Britain, capital growth of property has averaged 10% per year compound. This is despite many wars and the great depression.

For short-term property traders, negotiating a bargain price, finding the best interest rate and deciding when to buy and when to sell are extremely important. With long-term property investment, initial price, interest rate and timing are of less consequence because of the levelling effect of time. Thus, the best time to invest in long-term income-producing residential property is now. Time is always on your side.

To build up a successful property portfolio, you need to formulate and stick with a consistent investment policy. The formula developed in this book is to buy residential investment property that is appropriately financed to achieve maximum tax benefits while you are still working. With continually increasing property values, you continually finance and re-finance so that your liabilities (debt level) increase with your assets. This ultimately produces for you a retirement package of residential properties which will continue to grow in value and produce a regular indexed income for your retirement years.

The strategy

Step 1 — Preparation for a property portfolio (now)

In order to embark on a program of buying and keeping residential investment property, you need the following four basic ingredients to succeed:

- **Understanding of basic financial principles**
  No investment program will work unless you adopt such basic financial principles as:
  - paying off your credit cards on time;
  - buying a new car only when absolutely necessary;
  - buying luxuries only after investment commitments have been met;
  - borrowing for appreciating assets.

- **Sound asset backing**
  You should at least have a large amount of equity in your own home (i.e. the market value of your home minus what you still owe) or preferably have finished paying it off. Your own home or cash that you have on hand can be used as a stepping stone to borrow further funds for property investment. Put your assets to work for you instead of sitting on them. Cash is not a pre-requisite for property investment.

- **Reasonable cash flow**
  Even people in relatively lowly paid jobs can achieve wealth through property investment. It is extremely difficult to save as fast or work as hard as property values will increase. If you try to ''save'' from your existing income, it is most likely you will go two steps forward and one step back (in the form of tax). With property investment, it is possible to go two steps forward and be three steps in front because you have both taxes and inflation working for you.

  People on lower incomes may thus have sufficient cash flow for property investment. It is true that negative gearing assists higher income earners more, but we consider property investment to be by far the most attractive option no matter what your income. For the time that you are working, you must push money into your property investments in the form of interest payments in order to reap the benefit of capital gains later. Remember, when you borrow to invest in property, there are two other people assisting you with the interest bill — the tenant and the taxman.

  Your commitment is only a small part of the overall interest bill, but the returns (in the form of future capital gains) are all yours.

- **Knowledge**
  It will be repeated often through this book that knowledge minimises risk and maximises gains. Be prepared to glean whatever information you can from bank managers, accountants and solicitors — just remember that they are

experts in their own field, and not property investment. Talk to as many other property investors and read as many books as you can. Do your own sums and stay in control yourself.

Step 2 — Creation of the property portfolio (0-10+ years)

With your own house paid off (or almost), you begin to collect other properties and increase your level of debt. It is far easier to buy investment properties than your first house, primarily because of the fact that the tenant and the taxman (while you are working) are assisting you. Further properties are acquired over a staggered period of time depending on the increased value of the properties and the increase in cash flow both from rents and your other income. Over a period of about 10 to 15 years, it may be possible to collect as many as 10 properties — even on an average wage. You will find that it is usually the cash flow which constrains you from purchasing further property. At this stage, you may have assets worth $2,000,000 (10 houses with a future value of $200,000 each if purchased at $80,000 now and with a capital growth of 10% per year). You may still owe $1,000,000 but lo and behold — your net worth is that magic figure of $1,000,000.

It may seem impossible but it's not. Unless you think big, you will never achieve big. Remember the old sayings "If you think you can or think you can't — you're right" or "If you keep on doing what you have been doing then you will keep on achieving what you've been achieving". Your goal does not have to be 10 houses but it is important to have a goal.

Step 3 — Management of the property portfolio (10+ years)

With your collection of houses now in place, you have the ability to sell, stay static, or continue to buy more property, depending on your age and your expectations at this stage. Selling one or two properties may reduce the debt sufficiently for you to work part-time or even retire. Selling a house may provide sufficient funds for the new car and the overseas holiday. You are in control and the choice is yours. It is very important to note that superannuation funds may not pay you lump sums on retirement in the future (see Section 2.1). By creating your own superannuation fund in the form of property, you are able to "cash in" whenever YOU wish.

Step 4 — Retirement (10+ years)

At this stage your property portfolio becomes your primary source of income. To increase this source of income, you may need to reduce your level of debt by either selling some of your properties to clear the debt on others, or by using work-related superannuation monies to reduce or service the debt. Having realised your goal of "x" houses, you should now be in the comfortable position of being totally financially secure.

Consider what the situation would be if your goal was to achieve four houses, each worth $80,000 free of debt and rented at $140/week (note that these figures are in today's dollars, but projected to some time in the future, these would have the same purchasing power as the amounts listed here). This could provide:

— direct income of about $23,000/year clear of expenses (20%) and
— further capital growth of about $32,000/year (10% per year).

Thus your total "income" is $55,000, **plus** it is indexed for inflation as rents continue to increase and capital growth continues at 10%. If you compare this $55,000 to the current pension (around $8,800), you should be smiling. Just think what 10 properties would do for you! You have total control of what becomes of the properties — you may wish to sell them one at a time at various intervals or you may choose to keep them all so that your children may benefit from them.

Section 2. Residential Property — Your Doorway to Wealth

2.1 Why bother to invest?

The path of minimal resistance when it comes to investing is to do nothing. Statistics speak for themselves and the table below clearly demonstrates that only a small percentage of New Zealand's population will be likely to achieve total financial independence.

What will have happened to 100 young persons by the age of 65?

24	–	dead;
54	–	on the old-age pension;
16	–	still working;
5	–	financially independent;
1	–	wealthy.

Investment can be equated with financial freedom and puts you in control of your life. It is often said that money is the root of all evil, but for those without it and who need it, it is the root of an even greater evil. Below are the facts and fallacies which should be considered when you are deciding whether to invest at all and, if so, just how much you will need.

- **New Zealand's Aging Population**
  In 1920, less than 4% of New Zealanders were over 65 years of age. By 1980, it had increased to 11% and by 2020, it is estimated that about 18% of the population will be over 65. Increased medical technology enabling increased longevity has far outpaced society's willingness and ability to pay for such an aging population. No Government can support 18% of its population in a manner that they may want and, unless individuals are able to support themselves, there could be a drastic decline in living standards both for pensioners and for the rest of the population (who must pay more tax). It is estimated that by 2020, one welfare recipient will be supported by one taxpayer.

- **Income Level**
  It is a fallacy that you need lots of money to make lots of money. Net worth is not simply a function of income – it is just as much a function of planning. Many of today's high income earners cannot afford to stop working simply because they have not diverted sufficient income into building assets which would now be working for them. In contrast, many of today's wealthiest people were yesterday's lower-

income earners who followed basic financial principles. We become too entrenched in the idea that obtaining real wealth is beyond our capabilities because we, too often, associate wealth with a high income. Just remember, money comes from just three places – (1) people working; (2) money working; and (3) the Government. When you stop working, unless you have your money working for you, there is only one other option – the Government old-age pension.

- **Superannuation**
  If you think $200,000 is sufficient superannuation for a comfortable retirement, consider the fact that $200,000 invested at 10% (after tax), spent at the basic wage rate of $25,000 per year, and with inflation eroding what it will buy at the rate of 10% per year, will completely run out in just nine years. The same figures apply if you are expecting $500,000 in 10 years time. By then, the basic cost of living will be almost $60,000 per year and your lump sum will still run out in nine years. It is apparent that Government policy is to gradually phase out lump sum payments and instead convert them to annuities. To rely solely on superannuation is to lose control of your money when you need it most. Facts show that about 25% of people who reach 65 years of age are still working, mostly because they have to – not because they want to. In many cases, these are people who have retired at 55 with a tidy lump sum of $200,000 but by age 65, have found that it has "run out" (normal superannuation is further discussed in Section 2.2 in relation to property investment).

- **Life's Necessities**
  The public hospital systems are no longer free, and furthermore current waiting times for optional surgery are up to three years. Having medical facilities available when *you* want them costs you money. The State may provide free education, but if you would like the option of private school education for your children, it costs money. The Government ensures that all people are housed – but if you want to build that dream house just minutes for where you work, again it costs money.

2.2 What are the options?

Attributes of a good investment

The three main options available to the investor are *cash*, *shares* and *property*. In deciding just where you should be putting your investment dollar, first consider the main attributes of a good investment: *High capital growth*; *High security*; *Readily cashed*; *Tax advantages*; *Regular income*; *You maintain control*. On the next page is a comparison of the three main investment options (cash, shares and property) based on these attributes.

- **High capital growth**

  Cash   — No capital growth

  Shares   — The upward trend of the share market over the last 100 years has been estimated at around 6% compound per year.

  Property — Capital growth of property in New Zealand over the last 100 years has averaged just over 10% compound per year. In Great Britain, capital growth has averaged almost 10% per year over the last 900 years (records extracted from the Domesday Book of 1086).

- **High security**

  Cash   — Fairly safe, but depends on where you put it.

  Shares   — Banks will generally only accept about 25% of the face value of shares as a form of security. What does that tell you?

  Property — In contrast with shares, banks will accept up to 90% of the property value as a form of security (i.e. mortgage). What could be more secure?

- **Readily turned into cash**

  Cash   — Not usually a problem, except when you are locked into long-term deposits.

  Shares   — Not usually a problem, except that the more volatile nature of the share market means that timing can be critical.

  Property — Not a problem, though this may surprise a few people as the property market, like any market, is not always buoyant. In contrast with shares, you do not need to sell property to obtain cash as you can borrow against the equity. Most banks are only too willing to advance you cash if they hold the property as security.

- **Tax advantages**

  Cash   — None at all. Quite the reverse as you pay tax on the interest.

  Shares   — In some cases, "dividend imputation" can provide tax relief.

  Property — Excellent. Total deductibility of paper losses (negative gearing) is one of the big advantages of properly financed investment property.

- **Income**

  Cash   — Very reliable and a good source of direct income, but it is not indexed for inflation.

  Shares   — Unreliable. Companies do not always pay dividends on a regular basis as it depends on the operating profits (or losses) and plans for expansion.

  Property — Tenants in residential housing usually provide a steady reliable source of income that is indexed for inflation.

- **You maintain control**

  Cash   — You may have control of which financial institution that you "lend" your money to, but you have no control whatsoever over where it is invested.

  Shares   — You transfer control of your money to company directors or fund managers who invest your money the way that they want.

  Property — With direct investment in residential property, you stil maintain complete control over your investment. If, on the other hand, you simply put it in a property trust, then as with shares, you are transferring control to someone else.

From the above, it would seem that property is the only option that can claim to have all the attributes of a good investment. It is necessary to have some cash in reserve but with no capital growth and no tax advantages, it is not the best primary vehicle for building wealth. On the other hand, shares do offer capital growth and tax advantages, but their volatility does not make them a secure pathway to wealth and they become a "when-to" investment i.e. you must know when to buy and when to sell.

Comparison of rates of return

To get a true comparison of the real rate of return on alternative investments, they should always be reduced to the *after-tax* rate of return. For example, if you are in the top tax bracket and paying 33 cents in the dollar, then money in a bank account receiving 9% interest (which at first glance appears very attractive) would not be as rewarding as say 10 year insurance bonds paying 8% *after-tax*. The equivalent after-tax bank interest rate is calculated by:

After-tax interest rate = Pre-tax interest rate − (pre-tax interest rate × tax rate)

$$= 9.0 - (9.0 \times .33)$$
$$= 9.0 - 3.0$$
$$= 6.0\%$$

This means that if you invest $100,000 at 9% and receive $9,000 in interest, $3,000 is paid in tax and your "real interest" is only $6,000.

If you invest in investment products like insurance bonds or even superannuation funds, it is highly likely that your money will end up in investment properties. However, the returns on your investment are significantly reduced by all of the various middle men operating between your money and the property. This may take all of the effort out of investing, but it also takes all of the cream. One of the main reasons that direct property investment can offer such a high rate of return is because there are no salesmen, insurance company directors, or fund managers who must be paid from your profits.

The rate of return on your investment is determined by the amount of effort you put in. Even when you have selected an investment property, the returns can be increased depending on the effort you put into financing, improving and managing your property.

The after-tax returns on property investment can be greatly increased through the leverage effect of borrowed money as demonstrated in Section 5. The principle of leverage is elementary physics. With a lever, it is possible for a person to move and control large objects. Similarly with property investment, it is possible to control a large amount of property through leverage (i.e. DEBT). Investing in property without debt will preserve your investment in line with capital growth and the returns will be around 15%. With borrowed money, a great deal more property can be purchased and the returns can be levered to as much as 50%.

Rates of return for investment property can be calculated in several different ways. Capital growth, net yield, and return on deposit are the more usual methods of calculating these returns but they do not take taxation factors into account. A much better method which is used by most financial analysts is called the internal rate of return (IRR) — see Section 5. A brief description of each method is as follows:

- Capital growth = Increase in value/property value
  For residential property, this is about 10% compound per year.

- Net yield = Net rent/property value
  For residential property, this is approximately 6-7%.

- Return on deposit = increase in value/initial deposit
  It is quite meaningless to calculate a return on deposit when the deposit is nil.

- Internal rate of return (IRR)
  This combines the capital growth, yield, return on deposit, return on all cash outlays and tax advantages to produce an after-tax rate of return on the cash flow. In Section 5, we will show you how it is possible for the rate of returns on investment property to be in excess of 50% after-tax. To do this, we have developed a computer program available from de Roos Associates which produces a spreadsheet showing the projected capital growth, cash flow and real rate of return for an investment property.

Comparison of property investment with normal superannuation

Because long-term property investment is the equivalent of a personal superannuation scheme, it is worthwhile comparing its attributes to those of more conventional work-related superannuation schemes. Although these conventional superannuation schemes may also invest a large portion of their funds in property, their overall performance rarely reaches that of direct property investment in either rates of return (for the reasons mentioned earlier in this section) or flexibility (as outlined below).

Attribute	Conventional Superannuation	Direct Property Investment
Rate of return	8 — 15%	15 — 50%
Maximum lump sum	Maximum lump sum payments are typically limited to 25% of the accrued value (the rest being paid as annuities)	Unlimited
Maximum tax deduction	There is presently no deductibility for contributions to superannuation funds	Unlimited
Control over funds	The fund manager has complete control over where your funds are invested	You have complete control
Access to funds	With most schemes you cannot get access to your full entitlement until at least age 55. By resigning, you **may** be able to collect your contribution plus interest	You are able to sell properties or borrow against your equity in them at any time

2.3 Why residential property?

Once you have come to the conclusion that property is your best investment option, you must decide on the type and features of the property in which you are to invest.

Property Types

There are many types of investment available to the investor and all factors relating to the attributes of a good investment must be considered when deciding on your options. The main types of property are commercial, industrial, retail, hospitality, vacant land, rural, and residential.

- **Commercial**
- **Industrial**   These four types of property are commonly
- **Retail**   grouped together as commercial property.
- **Hospitality**

Commercial properties possess all the attributes of a good investment and can experience very high rent yields compared to residential. To your advantage, the tenant pays all the outgoings (rates, etc.) and will usually take a great deal of pride in keeping the building looking attractive for his own business purposes. However, commercial property should be reserved for those investors who possess a clear understanding and knowledge of the following:

- the business operation of the tenant and how economic downturns will affect vacancy rates (and consequently your cash flow);
- the pricing structure of commercial property;
- the suitability of the location for the particular tenant's needs;
- internal fittings required by prospective tenants;
- lease arrangements;
- risks beyond your control (e.g. Will a new shopping complex in the neighbourhood affect your tenant's business?)

Many investors have been highly successful in commercial property investments but you should note that a great deal more effort is needed to continually monitor and assess all of the risks, particularly those factors relating to the vacancy rate. The fact that 80% of small businesses do not survive their first year of operation further emphasises the high turnover of tenants in many commercial properties.

- **Vacant land**
  Good prime land can sometimes experience strong capital growth greater than 10% per year. But because it is not producing any income, any expenses associated with it (including that of interest on the borrowings) are not tax deductible against income from other sources. Consequently, the attractive tax benefits which are available to income producing property through negative gearing are lost with investment in vacant land.

- **Rural**
  If based on an income from farming etc., rural property can provide some tax benefits. However, because the yields are usually very low and the risks very high, it is generally only speculative development companies who are able to hold on to such low income producing property in anticipation of future re-zoning prospects.

- **Residential**
  Many investors avoid residential property simply because it is not glamorous; they would prefer to own the office block or bank building on the corner rather than the weatherboard house down the road. However, it is important to realise that good investment returns are not necessarily associated with glamorous exteriors. In contrast with commercial property, *residential property is for all investors* because everyone has an understanding of peoples' housing needs and the value of residential real estate (not everyone is able to gauge the business potential or the price of

the corner office block). The two basic requirements of man are food and *shelter*. Even in poor economic conditions when commercial property may be experiencing high vacancies, people must still live somewhere. The vacancies associated with residential property are usually so low that they do not drastically affect the cash flow. In addition, residential property encompasses all the features of a good investment (i.e. capital growth, security, easily turned into cash, tax advantages, provides income, and you still maintain control).

The fact that more money is invested in residential property than all other areas combined (see the table below) gives an indication of the magnitude of the market.

Total estimated value of:	$ Billion
1. New Zealand Trading Banks	14
2. Retail turnover per year	19
3. Retail property	23
4. Commercial property	26
5. Share market	28
6. Residential property	158

Residential property is our preferred option and is central to the strategy of buying and keeping investment property for your future financial security.

Which particular residential property?

Although there are many features to consider before choosing a particular property, your own discretion must play a large part in your final decision. Many property investors prefer flats while others prefer units or houses. Although the returns on multi-tenanted flats may be higher than on single units or houses, it is ultimately a matter of choosing what suits your personality.

Another factor that should determine whether you invest in houses, units or flats is the area: in the outer suburbs, families prefer to rent houses, while close to town, professional couples prefer units and professional singles may prefer a group tenancy in a large house. Flats may be suitable to rent to lower income earners in either the city or suburbs. Thus, to a large extent, you should always keep in mind just who is going to rent it (e.g. young professionals in the city or families in the suburbs).

Below is a list of features which may or may not apply, depending on price or location (e.g. a one-bedroom house on a small allotment on a busy road may be a good investment if it can be obtained for half the market price).

- **Location**
  Which town: A capital growth of 10% or more may be achievable in most areas where there is a stable economy. For this reason, cities and large provincial areas are preferable to country towns where the economy is based on a single factor

(e.g. the economy and therefore your property value may fluctuate depending on the price of a single commodity).

Which suburb: There is an element of luck in selecting the suburb which will return you substantially higher growth than the usual 10%. As a general rule, choose your property within a 15km radius of where you live, the main reason being your familiarity with house prices.

Which facilities: In general, tenants dislike houses which have the following detractions:

- on a busy road
- bus stop at front gate
- unsealed road
- next door to schools
- adjacent to industrial sheds
- across the road from a large sporting complex
- railway at back fence
- large shopping complex next door
- next door to public toilets

Properties which are well located in terms of capital growth and suitability for tenants should have a minimum of the above detractions and generally speaking should be "handy", but not necessarily "prime" (i.e. it is not necessary for a property to be one street back from the shopping centre so long as it is handy to transport, schools, shops, parks, and areas of employment).

- **Price**
  For flats and rental-units, the value of the property may be reasonably ascertained by capitalising the net return at whatever is the current acceptable rate (anywhere between 6 and 12%). For example, a block of flats returning $22,000 when others in the same area have been showing an 11% net return would have a capitalised value of $22,000 / 11%) = $200,000.

  Note that the rent for houses is not necessarily proportional to the house price: a $300,000 property does not usually rent for three times the rental of a $100,000 property. For this reason, it is advisable to look for properties in the bottom quarter of the market.

- **Type**
  When making a choice between brick, weatherboard, rough cast, or concrete block, it is necessary to consider both the maintenance factor and the price. For example, a weatherboard house bought for $75,000 may prove to be just as good an investment as an $85,000 brick dwelling.

- **Condition**

  Make sure that the property is structurally sound. A building inspection may be worth your while.

- **Size**

  Inner city properties may vary from one bedroom flats to six bedroom villas. In the suburbs, the most desirable properties tend to be houses with three bedrooms. Again the choice is up to your own judgement and will depend on the location and the market to which you are renting.

- **Car accommodation**

  It may suffice to have off-street parking with inner city properties but it is usually better for suburban properties to have a garage or at least a carport.

- **Fencing**

  Fully fenced is desirable in suburbia.

- **Aspect**

  Living rooms, lounges and dining rooms should be away from the southern side (preferably to the north).

- **Inside**

  The presence of curtains makes renting much easier, as do built-in wardrobes, or, in the case of an older house, one or two wardrobes supplied by the landlord.

- **Furniture**

  Unfurnished is preferable because tenants tend to treat your house with the same respect as they treat their own furniture. In addition, tenants tend to move less frequently because of the extra effort and expense involved in shifting their furniture.

- **Section size**

  At least 500 square metres in suburbia; inner city sections may be smaller and usually are.

- **Landscaping**

  Easy to mow lawns are ideal. While it is nice to have some trees and shrubs, tenants do not wish to spend every hour of the weekend trimming trees and maintaining gardens. Similarly swimming pools can be a hassle for both you and the tenant.

- **Zoning**

  Be aware of the zoning (residential, rural, etc.). Different councils have different regulations and these could substantially limit or enhance your options at a later date; however, don't speculate on possible re-zonings.

- **Rental level**

  Compare the rent value to the prevailing market rental for comparable dwellings (check with a letting agency if necessary). A rental level higher than the market rental may not be sustainable, while a significantly lower rental may enable you to increase the rent and thus the property value (which is based on rent).

- **Emotion**

  Do not become emotionally involved with your investment property. If you have assessed the property as being excellent except for the purple curtains which really turn you off, or you don't like the look of the neighbour's dog, go with the figures. If you are buying long-term, most of these things won't be around after a few years.

A typical residential investment property

A typical suburban investment house in a New Zealand city might be an eight-year old, three-bedroom brick house of about 90 square metres on a section of about 600 square metres. It would be fully fenced, have a carport and be situated in a reasonably quiet street. One of the bedrooms would have built-in wardrobes and the house would have both curtains and carpets throughout.

2.4 Building Wealth Through Residential Property

Although becoming a millionaire may be beyond the mental comprehension of most people, many do not realise that it is well within their reach, simply by following a strategy of long-term investment in residential property. But to achieve millionaire status, it is important to follow a strict but simple formula:

- Borrow against the equity in existing assets to purchase income-producing investment property.

- Do not sell the property in the short term for the sake of realising a cash profit.

- Borrow against the increased value to re-invest in further property in accordance with the ability to service the debt.

When you are striving to be financially successful, remember that your net worth is far more important than your income – **build wealth not taxable income**. To understand how these principles apply to residential property, consider the following example of building a residential property portfolio over a ten year period. (For simplicity, we will ignore the costs associated with purchasing and borrowing).

Year 0
Let us take the case of someone who owns a home worth $100,000 which we will use as the base from which to build the property portfolio. (It is important to note that we could have started equally well with someone who has only say $40,000 equity, as long as they have sufficient income to service the greater debt.)

Year 1
Two properties are purchased, each costing $100,000. This is achieved by using the principal residence and one of the investment properties as collateral for a $200,000 loan. Even though assets now total $300,000, net worth is still only $100,000.

Year 3
After a few years with capital growth at around 10% per year, when the properties have each increased in value to $130,000 (while the debt remains at $200,000) and income (rent and salary) has increased through inflation, two further properties are bought for $130,000 each. Total assets at this stage would be $650,000, and total debt would be $460,000, leaving a net worth of $190,000. The process may seem to be moving very slowly in the first few years and it is at this stage that many would-be investors sell up. But for those that hold, the magic of compound growth begins to have a dramatic effect.

Year 6
Two more properties each worth $180,000 are bought with additional borrowings, bringing the total debt to $820,000. By this stage, total assets have reached $1,260,000 and thus net worth has grown to $440,000 (still less than halfway to a million dollars after six years).

Year 10
With compound growth acting on the total assets but the debt remaining constant, growth in net worth is dramatic. By this stage, the total value of the seven properties has grown to $1,820,000 while the debt has remained at $820,000. Thus the goal of a net worth of $1,000,000 has been achieved.

The concept of being constantly in debt and "never owning anything" must be put in its true perspective. *It is not what you owe that is important, but what you own* (i.e. your net worth). Having achieved your goal, you would now have the option of continuing the process for as long as you wish or alternatively, reducing the debt (by selling a house or two) to increase your disposable income. Note that you need only sell three properties (total value of $780,000) to eliminate most of the $820,000 debt.

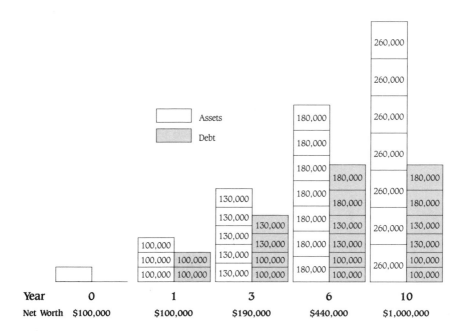

The above example is intended to outline the principles involved in building your wealth through residential investment property. Although the capital growth rate is shown as a constant 10% each year, in reality this is not the case – property values tend to increase in cycles. In some years, growth may be nothing, while in others it may be as much as 40 or 50%. But long-term property investment has the effect of ironing out the hills and troughs in the market cycles. For example, the value of one of our properties increased from $50,000 to $56,000 between 1984 and 1987 – an annual growth of 3.8%; but in the next three years annual growth increased to an average 16.7% such that, by 1990, the property had increased in value to $89,000. However, if growth is calculated over the whole 14 year period that we have owned the property, it works out to an average annual growth rate of 10.0%. The long-term average in property growth in New Zealand has actually been about 11%. Of course this may vary from location to location: some areas will have experienced sustained compounding growth rates much higher than this.

Section 3. Finance is the Key

Optimal financing is one of the most important keys to successful property investment. If you spend two days finding your investment property, then you should spend two weeks sorting out the finance. As we hope that you will eventually come to realise, you are not buying an investment property so much as a vehicle to financial security. An understanding of the basic financial principles involved will enable you to minimise your risks and to maximise your returns.

Once you have fully understood all of the ramifications of financing residential rental investment property, you will understand how you can be comfortable and still sleep, despite having what might seem, at first glance, an insurmountable debt. Having understood the opportunity cost in optimal financing, the most successful property investors would not be able to sleep at night if they were NOT in debt. We would like to relate to you the conversation between two young boys. One young fellow, dressed in shabby clothes, lamented to the other that his family were so poor that his dad owed the bank $2,000. The other boy, well dressed and proud of it, replied that his family were so rich that his dad owed the bank $2,000,000 and was about to borrow even more. The moral of the story states a fact of life today: most people who have achieved great wealth have done so by using other people's money.

Sorting out the financial maze can be a daunting task and is an area where professional advice in the initial stages can pay for itself 100 times over. There are many facets to contend with, each with numerous options, and everyone's situation is unique. The main points to consider are outlined as follows:

3.1 **Creative use of collateral**

3.2 **How much should you borrow?**

3.3 **What are the costs**

3.4 **Sources of finance**

3.1 Creative Use of Collateral

Before any financial institution will lend you a large amount of money, they require a security or collateral, which is your guarantee that you will repay the money. Usually this is by way of a mortgage on the property but, in many cases, insurance bonds may be used as security for a loan. It is the creative use of mortgages that can greatly improve the returns from your property investment portfolio. You do not need large amounts of cash up front to invest in property. You need a combination of existing assets and income. The assets you have are used as your base for borrowing and your income is used to service the loan. You are effectively diverting income into an asset building program.

The manner in which your assets are used as collateral to any borrowing is just as important as deciding where to borrow and is a most under-estimated part of many property investors' considerations. This becomes most important after you have purchased three or four properties and are about to buy more. If you have not set up your mortgages appropriately early on, it may prove costly to re-arrange. Be flexible, think laterally, and consider the following points:

- **Loans and Tax**

  For tax purposes, it is NOT the asset mortgaged that is relevant, but the USE to which the loan is put. Thus the interest on a loan against your primary place of residence can be tax deductible, as long as the loan funds are used to purchase an income producing investment – such as a rental property. It is very common to find people in a situation where they have paid off their first home and decide to go up-market to their dream home. They decide to keep their first home for investment (because they have seen just how good an investment it has been) and borrow money against it to build their new home. They then have an investment house with a mortgage – but the mortgage is NOT tax deductible because the purpose of the loan was to build their new house and not to finance income-producing investment property. The solution is usually to sell their first home, build the new house with the proceeds and borrow against their new house to buy an investment property. The situation is then that their principal place of residence now has a mortgage on it but the purpose of the loan is to buy an investment property. The interest on the loan in this case is fully tax deductible.

- **Loan/value ratio**

  Get maximum mileage from loan/value ratios. In other words, don't give the financial institution any more security than they need. Some institutions charge mortgage insurance. This is an insurance paid by you. If you fail to meet the obligations of the loan, the mortgagee can sell your property and claim from the mortgage insurers any shortfall between the loan and the selling price (it differs from income insurance which is your insurance against reduced income). Be careful when you are refinancing properties and having them revalued by valuers contracted by lending institutions. Values rarely come up to your expectations (valuers tend to be overly conservative – see "valuations" later in this section) and it can result in a lower loan than anticipated. Note that, although you may borrow the entire amount for your investment property by using other property as collateral, it is a good idea to keep your overall asset:debt ratio at 2:1.

- **Deposits**

  Cash "deposits" are not needed if other collateral can be used in conjunction with the loan. For example, if you own your own home, you can use this as security for your next investment property. There is no need to "save up a deposit" for that property.

- **Mortgage flexibility**

  Don't take out an inflexible mortgage on a house you may want to sell. If you do mortgage your principal place of residence with an inflexible mortgage (i.e. high penalties if you want out), make sure that you intend staying for the period of the loan. If a job transfer is imminent, make different arrangements regarding the collateral or take out a more flexible loan.

- **Second mortgage**

  Consider a second mortgage. The idea of a second mortgage is foreign to most people because it is usually associated with "being on the brink of insolvency". This is simply not the case as second mortgages can be very effective in many cases and less expensive than paying mortgage insurance. For example, if you are lucky enough to have an old War Service loan of $50,000 at 5% and your property is now worth $150,000, it would be silly to refinance the loan to another finance institution who wants a first mortgage in order to give you $70,000 (20,000 + 50,000 refinanced War Service loan) at 10% interest. Your total interest bill would be $7,000. If you obtained a second mortgage at 16%, your total interest bill would only be $5,700 (5% of 50,000 + 16% of 20,000).

- **Unencumbered property**

  An unencumbered property is one that is not secured by any mortgage documentation as security for a loan. The property may have been bought using a loan (mortgaged to another property) but it is free and clear and can thus be mortgaged for further property acquisition. For example, if your principal place of residence is valued at $150,000 and mortgaged at $100,000 to purchase an investment property for $95,000 (the additional $5,000 is used for costs), the investment property has not been mortgaged and is still unencumbered. Your principal place of residence is encumbered (mortgaged) but the purpose of the loan was for the investment property and so is tax-deductible.

  Try to keep at least one property unencumbered to maintain a degree of flexibility, though this may be difficult in the early stages of building your property portfolio.

- **Multi-property mortgages**

  Don't tie up more than two or three properties on the one mortgage document as it may be costly to release a particular property from the mortgage. It is slightly more expensive to request individual mortgages on individual properties but it may save you a lot of time and expense in the future.

- **Deed of variation of loan**

  When property values rise, consider a "deed of variation of loan". This involves having the properties revalued and borrowing against the increased equity to buy more property on the same mortgages.

- **Cash contracts**

  Cash contracts can be very attractive to vendors and it is worthwhile arranging finance before signing a contract (by using other property as security or by having it pre-approved on the prospective property, or simply using cash). Signing a contract "subject to finance" in the hope that it is a way out is not a sound arrangement in today's financial world as finance is relatively easy to obtain.

- **Valuations**

  Always remember the lending institution's value is invariably lower than market value (they work on the basis of having to recoup their money within two months). Valuations can affect how much you will be able to borrow when re-financing.

- **Name**

  The name of the person(s) with title to the property being *mortgaged* is not important for tax purposes. But what is critical for tax purposes is the name of the person with title to the property being *purchased*. Properties bought with tax relief in mind, should be bought in the name of the highest income earner, while property bought for income should be bought in the name of the lowest income earner. Properties bought in a *company name* warrant special mention. If you must borrow substantially on your own property which is not tax deductible, buying the house in your company name and renting back can reduce your company's (and hence your) tax burden.

- **Mortgage Power**

  Loans which enable you to use your collateral as you would a cheque book are great in certain circumstances. The way they work is that you give the bank a mortgage on a particular property for a loan facility which then enables you to draw against the account or pay back the loan at your discretion, provided it does not go over the limit. They are great for having a ready source of cash and picking up "bargains" through cash contracts, but not so great for long-term property investments as the interest rates tend to be higher.

3.2 How much should you borrow?

Borrowing money enables you to build up capital more rapidly than otherwise would be possible, but how much you borrow depends on many factors which can be divided into two categories – your **capacity to borrow** and your **ability to manage the debt**. You can borrow nothing or the entire amount (including the borrowing and purchasing costs as well as the initial cash flow deficit) – whatever suits your own situation.

Borrowing capacity

- **The level of income from other sources**

  Initially, the excess cash flow from your regular job (your "earned income") and the rent are used to service the debt. As a general rule of thumb in determining the size of loan that you can service:

  Total interest = 30% of gross salary + 80% of gross rents

  This formula will apply to the majority of people who earn up to say $45,000 per year. Obviously, if your income is higher, you are able to commit a higher percentage of salary to servicing a loan – firstly because you have more funds available and secondly, because your tax savings are greater. Debt levels can be made to fluctuate depending on what income you require, and combinations of *income only, capital growth only*, or both *income and capital growth* can be obtained by manipulating the loans to suit. Once you have decided to retire, the substantial property portfolio that you have built up can be adjusted to suit your needs and it may be desirable to simply adjust the debt accordingly. Generally, the ratio of total assets to debt should be about 2:1, although this is not always possible in the initial stages.

- **Your marginal rate of tax**

  The interest on large borrowings can be used to offset higher income from other sources and reduce the overall tax quite significantly (negative gearing). The higher the marginal rate of tax, the larger the tax relief.

- **Other properties used as security**

  When other properties are available as collateral for the loan, then it may be possible to borrow the entire amount of the purchase price (i.e. no cash deposit may be necessary). You may borrow "bits and pieces" of money from several properties using a combination of first and second mortgages, deeds of variation of mortgage and mortgage power loans.

- **Your age and retirement expectations**

  As you approach retirement, you should be planning towards having your rental income replace your "earned salary". To achieve this, you may need to stop buying further properties and to reduce your debt levels and interest payments by selling some of your existing properties. Once your primary source of income reduces, so do the tax advantages of high debt levels. However, you can continue to manipulate the tax simply by manipulating the debt level. Remember, you are in control.

- **Anticipated rate of return**

  The level of borrowing can ultimately determine the real rate of return. In general the higher the debt level, the higher the rate of return (see Section 5).

- **Rental income**
  Over a period of time, rental income from your existing properties should increase with inflation. This increased income provides funds to service additional borrowings.

Debt management

Your ability to manage a large debt is paramount to your success as a long-term property investor and will enable you to ride through any market cycle hiccups. The following points should also be considered when determining how much to borrow.

- **Cash reserves**
  Always keep sufficient cash reserves on hand to allow for unforeseen expenses such as a temporary drop in primary income (changing jobs) or rental vacancies.

- **Credit cards**
  Obtain as many cards as you can so that you have instant access to funds should the need arise. Don't use them to splurge on consumables not associated with your investment properties.

- **Rent cycles**
  Keep a close watch on rent cycles and be prepared to lower the rent to reduce vacancies.

- **Assets : liability ratio**
  Try to maintain the overall assets : liabilities ratio at 2:1 (this may not be possible in the initial stages).

- **Unreliable income**
  Don't commit unreliable income (e.g. overtime) to interest payments. In the case of a two-income family, do not commit both incomes to interest payments if there is the possibility that one might stop work in the immediate future (e.g. to start a family).

- **Speculation**
  Do not speculate on the possibilities of rent increases or interest rate reductions. As a guide, budget for three years at present income levels.

- **Partnerships**
  Avoid partnerships where possible. Business deals with friends can be a recipe for lost friendships.

- **Knowledge**
  Keep up with the pursuit of knowledge. Financial worry is caused by the lack of knowledge.

- **Time**
  Do not be concerned about the time it takes for your assets to grow. The level of debt that you currently possess will, in ten years, be a small proportion of your overall assets. Put your debt in a long-term, not a short-term, perspective.

- **Budget**
  The key to debt management is working out a budget, taking all of the above points into consideration, and then sticking to it. It means buying luxuries only after your debt commitments have been met.

- **Other factors**
  There are numerous factors which affect your ability to feel comfortable with a large property investment debt. Many of these are discussed in Section 7.

3.3 What are the costs?

The costs involved with an investment property must be considered before you decide where to borrow your funds. These include both the borrowing costs and the purchase costs.

Borrowing Costs

Borrowing costs associated with loans can be divided into two categories: those charged by financiers and standard Government charges. These costs are tax deductible (see Section 4.1). It is difficult to sort out the maze when it comes to borrowing money. To make it easier, the following questions should be asked of each prospective financier (note that there are additional borrowing costs in the form of Government charges which are standard to all lending institutions).

- **What is the interest rate?**
  Interest rates should not be the sole criterion for choosing a loan. An interest of 11% may be cheaper than another at 10% when other factors are considered.

- **Is the interest fixed or variable?**
  Fixed interest loans are usually associated with inflexible type mortgages – once you're in, you're in. This may be very useful if you are buying for a long-term investment. Cash flow budgets are important to property investments and fixed interest rates allow for better budgeting and peace of mind. If interest rates are falling, however, it may be better to choose a variable rate. In some cases, it is possible to switch from a variable to a fixed rate but not vice versa.

  Whether you decide to take a variable or fixed rate of interest depends on your perception of the money market (something on which even economists can't agree) and your financial muscle (i.e. can your budget withstand any upward movement in interest rates). Three-year fixed interest rates are invariably more stable than either variable rates or short-term bank bills as indicated by the figures over the last ten years shown below.

1984-1994 Property Investment Loan Rates

Fixed 3 year rates	8.5 − 15%
Variable rates	7.5 − 16%
90 day bank bills	6 − 18%

- **Do they offer Principal and Interest or Interest-only loans?**

  A Principal and Interest (P & I) loan requires part of the loan to be paid back as well as the interest, usually each month, so that at the end of the term of the loan, it is completely paid off. Too many bank managers suggest short-term P & I loans to customers without explaining to them the important effects of taxation.

  The main disadvantages of a P & I loan are:

  - Money paid out on the principal part of the loan is not tax deductible.
  - Because the principal is reducing, the amount of interest also lessens. This reduces the total claims against rent and you begin paying more tax.
  - The larger monthly payment needed reduces your ability to fund further properties.
  - The extra principal payment is from after-tax dollars.

  Interest-only loans are usually best for servicing long-term property investments.

- **Is the interest calculated in arrears or advance?**

  Interest paid monthly in advance is approximately 0.2% dearer than monthly in arrears. The difference in the cost is simply the interest on the interest for the fraction of the year that you have use of the money before the interest is due. For example, one month in arrears at 15% is equal to $0.15 \times 0.15 \times (1/12)$, which is about 0.2% (i.e. 15% in advance is about 15.2% in arrears).

- **Is the interest calculated daily or monthly?**

  Daily is better than monthly because interest is only calculated on what you owe at any point in time. If you were to make a lump sum repayment at the beginning of a month on a loan where the interest is calculated monthly (if you had a P & I loan), you would effectively be giving the bank the loan of your money for a month interest-free.

- **How often is the interest paid?**

  If you have an interest-only loan, some lending institutions may be prepared to be flexible on the frequency of interest payments (i.e. monthly, quarterly or yearly). Consider the reverse situation; would you prefer to receive interest monthly (and get interest on your interest) or yearly? So too with borrowing money. It is better for you to pay a lump sum at the end of the year than monthly instalments.

Most banks do not offer this option and for those that do, the interest rate is adjusted accordingly. It may be tax advantageous to you to pay the interest fully in advance. If, at the end of the financial year, you realize you need tax relief, borrowing the money for a property and paying the interest 12 months in advance will reduce the tax liability for that year. It is worthwhile understanding this aspect.

- **How much are the establishment fees/application fees?**
These vary from 0 to 4% of the loan. This is the main trade-off in comparing interest rates. A loan with an interest rate of 14% and no application fee is suitable for a short term (which you don't want), while an interest rate of 11% fixed with a 1% application fee and no solicitor's fees may be more attractive for the long-term investor (that's you).

- **How much are the valuation fees?**
Some banks may charge nothing (being covered by higher interest rates) but the standard fee may be several hundred dollars for a house. This can vary depending on location, number of properties and whether or not it's a revaluation by the same firm.

- **How much are the mortgagee's solicitor's fees?**
Depending on the type of loan, mortgagee's solicitors occasionally charge fees for the preparation of the mortgage documentation. These fees may vary up to about $1,000 on a $100,000 loan.

- **Does the loan require mortgage insurance?**
Mortgage insurance has not been very common in New Zealand in the past, but some banks now require mortgage insurance on all loans. Others require it on loans only where the loan/value ratio is more than 75%. Mortgage insurance is paid only once for each term of the loan.

- **What is the maximum loan/value ratio?**
Many banks will not lend more than 75% of *their* valuation but their valuation is usually about 85% of the market value. Some will go as high as 95%. It is important to know how much you are able to borrow with a given property as it may be better to forego a lower interest on a loan with a company who will only lend to 60%, in favour of a slightly higher interest rate where the maximum loan/value ratio is 85%. Don't confuse the fact that you can borrow 100% on any one particular property. It is the overall total loan/value ratio which is limited. For example, if you use your principal place of residence (valued at $150,000) to purchase an investment property for $100,000, you may borrow 100% of the investment property, but the loan/value ratio is 100,000/150,000 or 66.6%.

- **What are the rules for determining borrowing capacity?**
Some rules that are intended for first home buyers who have not yet established their credibility may be stifling to your investment property program. If you take

control and show that you do not fit in with a bank's "30% of income and 80% of rent" rules, set out your own figures to show how you can afford the loan or go elsewhere. Most banks do not consider the great tax savings which can alter significantly the income at your disposal.

- **Are there penalties for early repayment?**
  With flexible loans, there may be no penalties. In other cases, the penalty may be as high as four months interest. If you are not sure how to arrange your mortgages, don't lock into a high penalty mortgage that is costly to refinance later.

- **How easy is it to transfer the mortgage to other securities?**
  In many cases, there may be a substitution of collateral (exchange the property being held as security) for only a small fee. It is worthwhile checking. A very small number of loans can be sold with the property though this is not common. These are referred to as "assumable" loans.

- **How much are the monthly and yearly charges?**
  There may be a small ($1 − $10) monthly fee which is fairly standard. The ones to watch for are the $200+ yearly charges.

- **How much is the brokerage fee?**
  Most brokers receive their fees from the lending institutions. Be careful to check whether you are dealing with a broker or directly with a lending institution (these are not distinguished in the "Finance-Mortgage Loans" Section of the phone book's yellow pages).

- **Is life insurance required?**
  This may be compulsory with some loans. It's probably a good idea to have life insurance but be sure that you are not coerced into taking out additional cover with the lender if it is not really needed.

- **What are the mortgage release fees?**
  A bank or lending institution may charge you additional fees for simply handing over the mortgage documents when the loan is paid out or re-financed. Such fees are usually within the range of $30 to $112.50.

- **How much are the rollover fees?**
  When you take out a fixed loan for a period of time (e.g. fixed or variable interest loans over three years), rolling over for a further period of time may cost money. The fee can be almost nothing or quite substantial (more than $1000), depending on whether solicitors are involved. Rollover fees are not applicable to P & I loans.

- **Do they offer an overdraft facility (e.g. Mortgage Power type)?**
  Can you pay it out and draw on it again at no cost? These can be very useful in some circumstances but because of the usually high interest rate, should not be used for long-term investment.

Example of borrowing costs

Typical borrowing costs on a loan of $101,989 to cover the full cost of a $100,000 property plus the associated purchasing costs (say $510) and the borrowing costs could be:

Establishment fee (1% of loan)	$1,020
Valuation fees	$ 300
Registration of mortgage (× 2)	$ 92
Registration of title	$ 46
Search fees	$ 21
	$1,479

Note: Depending on circumstances, search fees may be classified for tax purposes as either a borrowing cost or a purchasing cost (see Purchasing Costs).

Government charges associated with borrowing

In addition to the financier's costs, there are Government charges beyond the control of the financier and which are standard to all lending institutions:

- **Registration of Title** (arguably a purchase cost — currently $46)
- **Registration of Mortgage** (currently $46)

Purchasing Costs

The only variable cost in purchasing your property investment is your own solicitor's fees. The purchase costs are not tax deductible but must be capitalised and depreciated (see Section 4.3).

- **Stamp duty on purchase**
  Residential properties, including residential investment properties, are totally exempt from stamp duty. By comparison, commercial properties are charged stamp duty at the following rates:

Price / Value	Marginal Rate ($ / $100)
up to $50,000	1.00
from $50,000 to $100,000	1.50
excess over $100,000	2.00

- **Your solicitors fees**
  Your solicitor will charge for handling the transfer documents (conveyancing). Examples of typical solicitors' fees are:

Property Value	Solicitors Fees (inclusive of GST)		
	No Mortgage	One Mortgage	Two Mortgages
under $100,000	$495	$595	$665
$100,000-$200,000	$535	$645	$715
over $200,000	$575	$695	$765

Note that these fees do not include Government registration charges or search fees, for which an extra $100 should be allowed. It *is* possible to do the conveyancing and the searches yourself. The process is not complicated but is time consuming, mainly because of the number of forms involved. If you have any doubts at all, use a solicitor.

- **Search fees**
  There may be instances where these costs are considered for taxation purposes as a borrowing cost. This comes about because although you would want to have searches carried out before purchasing a property, the financial institution may **insist** that searches be carried out before they will lend any money. These fees are charged by the various government departments to provide you with necessary information and documentation (note that when a solicitor is responsible for your searches, you will be charged for his time as well). Search fees may vary, but typically cost from $10 to $40.

Selling Costs

The concept of buying to keep is further emphasised by the fact that selling costs can be quite significant. Should your program be at a selling stage, the following costs should be taken into account.

- **Sales commission**
  This varies between real estate firms, and is generally negotiable. As a rough guide for houses priced around $100,000, the commission is approximately 3%.

- **Your solicitor's fees**
  There is less work involved in selling than buying and solicitor's fees are consequently less. The fees may vary, but typical vendor's solicitor's fees are:

Property Value	Solicitors Fees (inclusive of GST)		
	No Mortgage	One Mortgage	Two Mortgages
under $100,000	$380	$460	$520
$100,000-$200,000	$420	$510	$570
over $200,000	$460	$560	$620

- **Mortgage release fees**
  This may be simply the cost of releasing the registered mortgage or it may include such costs as mortgagee's solicitor's fees ($\sim$$300+), mortgagee's re-arrangement fees ($\sim$$300+), and revaluation of other properties to allow release of one property from the mortgage ($\sim$$300). Most of these costs are tax deductible directly from income in the year of sale.

- **Hidden costs**
  Depending on the time it takes to sell a property (usually about three months), there may be an opportunity cost factor of lost rent; if tenants move out well in advance, this cost may be as high as $1800 ($150/week × 12 weeks).

3.4 Sources of finance

There are numerous options available when financing an investment property. Having carefully considered the main points to look for in a loan (see Section 3.3), you can then seek out the best source of finance. It is not always the best option to "bank where you have always banked". When making an application for a loan, make sure you have done your sums first. Set out your assets and liabilities statement and cash flow statement clearly so that you reassure the financier that you are in control of the situation. Ask for the amount that you want and know you can handle. Never ask "How much will you lend me?". There is no need to fabricate figures as it only leaves a black mark against your name *when* you are found out. Remember, the more assets and loans you have, the better will be your credit rating. The various sources of finance include: traditional banks, building societies/credit unions, trustee companies, finance companies, private finance, vendor finance, finance brokers, overseas finance, insurance companies, and international banks.

Generally speaking, the higher the interest rate, the higher degree of flexibility of the loan and conversely, the lower the interest rate, the lower degree of flexibility (i.e. once you are in, you are in, and it is difficult to either sell or alter the loan in any way without high penalties).

- **Traditional Banks** e.g. ANZ, BNZ, National Bank, Westpac
  These banks have undergone tremendous change in the last few years and are well worth considering. Their property investment loans tend to have modest up-front fees (i.e. low application and valuation fees), and they usually offer Mortgage Power type loans. If you like the comfort of a large bank and their flexible mortgages, this may be your choice.

- **Building Societies and Credit Unions**
  These are excellent for first home owners and also for property investors. They have fairly strict rules applying to income levels and are not usually flexible if you don't fit the guidelines – even though you can well afford the loan. They tend to have quite acceptable up-front charges.

- **Trustee Companies** e.g. Perpetual Trustees
  Their low interest rates and reasonably low up-front charges make them very attractive for long-term property investors. However, the mortgages are not usually flexible and there may be high penalty costs. If you are keeping properties long-term, then these shouldn't concern you. Once you have sorted out how to use your collateral, these companies can be a good source of finance for most of your borrowing needs.

- **Finance Companies**
  In general, they have almost non-existent up-front fees, but high interest rates. There are a few small finance companies which are exceptions and these tend to follow

the trustee company facilities. Finance companies are great for developers and traders in property where relatively short-term commitments lessen the impact of high interest rates.

- **Private Finance**
  Borrowings may be from family members or solicitors and accountants. It was fairly standard practice to borrow funds from solicitor's clients before deregulation of the financial markets made money access much easier. In some cases, it may not be necessary to pay any up-front fees at all.

- **Vendor Finance**
  Sometimes the vendor will carry back a first or second mortgage. But be wary – a low interest rate is usually coupled with a high purchase price.

- **Broker**
  Brokers receive their fees from the financial institutions. They occasionally have access to the superannuation funds and can sometimes secure you finance at a rate 0.5% lower than the best elsewhere.

- **Overseas Finance**
  Very low interest loans are possible but because of the fluctuating dollar, you could see yourself going backwards. Unless you are prepared to gamble or can hedge against a drop in the dollar, stay well clear.

- **Insurance Companies**
  It is possible to borrow money against the value of any life assurance policies you may have. Some insurance companies will lend you up to 90% of the amount and usually at competitive interest rates.

- **International Banks** e.g. Citibank, Chase
  These are usually innovative with their investment loans and often appear quite attractive. But check out all the possible angles – especially penalty rates – before deciding.

Section 4. Tax Implications

It is often said that there are only two things that are certain in this world – death and taxes. However, our Government does not simply collect taxes to keep itself financially afloat; the taxation laws are structured so as to provide both incentives and disincentives for various activities. The current tax laws in the area of property investment are so attractive that it would seem as if the Government is offering tax incentives to help solve the ''housing crisis''. In other words, by investing in property, you are doing exactly what the Government is encouraging you to do.

Property investment is all about building your wealth. Thus, it is necessary to understand all of the implications and ramifications of the current tax laws as they relate to property investment. The two main areas of taxation relating to property investment are: *tax deductions* and *negative gearing*.

4.1 Tax deductions

All expenses ''incurred in gaining assessable income'' are tax deductible, so maintain complete records of all expenses incurred. Don't take the risk of unsupported claims – document all of the costs as though it were a business (after all, it should effectively become a business operation). If you are not interested in working out the taxation details relating to your investment property, at least keep all of the documentation in an orderly fashion for your accountant. Don't simply provide him with a shoebox full of receipts and expect him to do the rest. It can cost you a fortune in accounting fees if you expect an accountant to attend to all the small details. Tax deductibility falls into two categories: *capital costs* and *revenue costs*.

Capital costs

These costs are *not* directly deductible against rental income but are capitalised (i.e. added to the capital cost of the property) and then depreciated. Capital costs include:

- **Purchase costs**
  Registration of Title (see Section 3.3) stamp duty on purchase (commercial property only) and that portion of your solicitor's fees that relate to conveyancing.

- **Improvement costs**
  There is a subtle but very important difference between improvements and repairs. Repairs are defined as those expenses which bring the property to its value when you bought it (not the original value when it was built). For example, if you buy a property which needs painting and re-roofing before it can be tenanted, the costs

are for improvement (i.e. capital costs) and not classed as repairs. Such costs can only be capitalised and depreciated. However, if you borrow money for these improvements, then the interest on those borrowings can be claimed directly. If a property is bought in good condition and needs painting and re-roofing four years later due to wear and tear, the costs would most likely be considered as repairs and therefore directly tax deductible. There is also a subtlety in doing "repairs". For example, if you re-roof an old rusted iron-roofed house with iron, it is considered a repair. But if you were to use tiles, it would be classed as an improvement.

- **Disposal costs**
These include sales commission and your solicitor's conveyancing fees on sale of the property.

Revenue costs

These costs are directly deductible against all other income. It is worthwhile noting that the actual cost (money from your hip pocket) is less than the paper costs (deductions you can claim) because of the inclusion of depreciation and borrowing costs. The total expenses, over and above interest in operating a residential property can be up to 25-30% of the gross rent. As a guide to the items you could claim, a list of typical deductions is set out below. These are based on a house purchased for $100,000 with borrowings of $101,989 (to cover purchasing and borrowing costs as well) at a fixed interest of 12.0%. Rent is $150 per week (grossing $7,800 per year).

Income

Gross rent			$7,800

Notes	Deductions	Paper Costs	Actual Costs
a.	Rates	$720	$720
b.	Insurance	$310	$310
c.	Interest on borrowings	$12,239	$12,239
d.	Borrowing costs	$1,479	paid for in loan
e.	Agent's commission (7.5% + 1 week's rent)	$735	$735
f.	Management fees (10% to spouse)	$780	$780
g.	Repairs	$150	$150
h.	Cleaning	$50	$50
i.	Gardening	$50	$50
j.	Depreciation (on building and chattels)	$2,950	artificial
k.	Advertising	$60	$60
l.	Telephone	$10	$10
m.	Stationery/postage	$8	$8
n.	Car (26 trips at 20km at 0.46c/km)	$239	$239
o.	Mower fuel	$10	$10
	TOTAL DEDUCTIONS	$19,790	$15,361

(See notes following for other possible deductions.)

Notes on tax deductions

a. Rates
All local authority charges, including water rates, general rates, rubbish collection, and sewerage.

b. Insurance
Do not skimp on insurance. It is a critical part of minimising investment risk and is a tax deduction as well. Building insurance should cover replacement value as well as lost rent, demolition fees, architects fees etc. Contents insurance should cover drapes and carpets if it is otherwise unfurnished.

c. Interest on borrowings
Money can be borrowed for the following:
- purchase
- borrowing and purchase costs
- cash flow deficit
- improvements
- repairs

If the loan is fixed-interest, interest-only, the amount will be constant each year. If the loan is principal and interest, then only the interest component of repayments is deductible and, because the principal is being paid off, the annual interest will decline.

d. Borrowing costs
These include ALL costs associated with the loan (application fees, valuation fees, mortgage insurance, mortgagee's solicitor's fees, search fees required by mortgagee, registration of mortgage, broker's fees, etc.).

e. Agent's commission
All fees for both letting and managing are deductible and usually amount to about 10% of the gross rent. Money withheld from a bond for repairs is treated as income. Your spouse may act as your agent.

f. Management fees
If your spouse does the banking, keeps the books, and organises the repairs, then a 10% management fee is acceptable. Many managers of holiday units charge fees in excess of 30%, so 10% is a reasonable figure.

g. Repairs
These include painting, fence repairs, re-tiling, roof-fixing – in fact, just about anything that can be classed as property maintenance, but check the distinction between repairs and improvements as previously outlined in this section on capital costs. The timing of repairs is critical for two reasons. Firstly, if you buy a run-down

house and then immediately paint it, carpet it, and put on a new roof, these activities would not be considered repairs, but improvements and thus are not deductible as such (you can claim the interest on any money borrowed for such work, and you can depreciate the improvements). Secondly, if you have genuine repairs to be done, then it is very tax-effective to have them done toward the end of your financial year.

h. Cleaning

This includes carpet cleaning etc. It is possible that your spouse could be employed to carry out these duties between tenancies.

i. Gardening

The cost of having the lawn mowed, trees trimmed, and gardens weeded can all be a deduction. Again, this is another area where members of the family have the opportunity to earn some pocket money.

j. Depreciation

Depreciation is the method of writing off the wear and tear on assets used to produce income. The depreciation rates are set by the Commissioner of Inland Revenue. Both chattels and buildings may be depreciated.

The two methods used for depreciation operate on the "Diminishing Value" (DV) basis and the "Straight Line" (SL) basis. Using the Diminishing Value basis, the depreciation for a given financial year is a fixed percentage of the written down or book value of the asset, where the book value is the original cost less the depreciation deducted in previous years. Using the Straight Line basis, the depreciation is a constant percentage of the original cost price so that the amount of depreciation remains constant each year.

• *Depreciation of chattles*
The cost of the item is the amount actually paid (or its assessed value) plus installation costs. When you first purchase a property, it is your responsibility to set a fair value on each of the items as they exist in the property at the time (not what they cost when new).

Example of chattel depreciation:
For carpet with an estimated value of $1,000

By D.V. method, 33% of diminished value can be claimed each year

Year 1	Year 2	Year 3	etc.
$330	$210	$152	etc.
	33% of ($1000 − $330)	33% of ($670 − $210)	

Below is a list of assets typically depreciated and their current depreciation rates.

Item	D.V. (%)	S.L. (%)
Curtains	22	15.5
Carpets	33	24
Fluorescent lights	18	12.5
TV sets	33	24
Refrigerator	22	15.5
Electric heaters	50	40
Washing machines	26	18
Stove	22	15.5

Note: Bedding, crockery, cutlery, linen, glassware and cooking utensils are claimed at *replacement value* – not depreciated.

When you have a number of houses, it is worthwhile claiming the depreciation for items that are used both privately and at your investment properties. This can be done on a separate depreciation schedule. In this case, simply reduce the amount of the deduction by a fraction equivalent to that of private use. Such items might include mowers, power tools, sewing machines (for curtains), computer, answering machine, ladders, wheelbarrow, etc. As a guide – if you have one investment property, 10% property and 90% private should be acceptable, while if you have 15 properties, 90% property and 10% private should be more appropriate.

• *Depreciation of buildings*
Depreciation of buildings refers solely to the capital improvements of the property, and therefore excludes the land (which theoretically does not depreciate in value) and the chattels (which are depreciated at different rates as outlined above).

The depreciation rate for properties bought after April 1st 1993 is either 3% Straight Line or 4% Diminishing Value.

Example of building depreciation:

Property cost (house + land)	=	$100,000
Land value	=	$40,000
House value including chattels	=	$60,000
Chattel value	=	$7,000
Capital improvements value	=	$53,000
Depreciation (assuming a wooden house)	=	3% of $53,000
	=	$1,590

- **Advertising**
  This may include newspaper advertisements to obtain tenants or tradesmen.

- **Telephone**
  Keep an accurate and detailed record of all calls for a period of time (e.g. three months) and work out the percentage relating to property compared to private use. You can then use this figure for all future claims until your situation changes.

- **Stationery/postage**
  All writing material and postage costs can be claimed.

- **Car**
  Make a habit of driving past each of your investment properties at least once a fortnight. If it looks good from the outside, it will probably be good on the inside.

  If you travel fewer than 5,000km per year on property related business, then you may claim according to the Inland Revenue Mileage Rates applying from April 1st 1996:

Distance per year	Rate per km
Up to 3000km	62c
3001-5000km	19c

  If you have a large number of properties and exceed 5,000km per year, then you may claim the rates specified above up to 5,000km only ($2,240) or the actual expenses incurred apportioned to the percentage of property related running over total annual vehicle running. In the latter case you will have to maintain log books to justify your claims.

- **Mower fuel**
  Pay for this separately when you are at the garage and get a receipt.

- **Heating and cooling**
  This may include the supply of wood or coal for a fireplace or any other heating or cooling system.

- **Bank charges**
  These may relate directly to your loan or you may claim a percentage of your cheque account/credit card charges according to the amount of business use.

- **Electricity**
  In most cases, this is the tenant's responsibility, but if not, you should claim it.

- **Hire charges**
  The hiring of trailers for rubbish removal and ladders for repair work on your investment properties are deductible.

- **Legal expenses**
  These include expenses for lease preparation, tenant eviction, etc.

- **Pest control**
  Depending on the terms of the lease, this may or may not be at the tenant's expense. If you pay for it, you can claim it.

- **Body corporate fees**
  These sometimes pertain to unit owners and will vary in cost from $3 upwards, depending on the rent and unit value. They normally include building insurance and will fund external repairs to the complex at a later date.

- **Mortgage release fees**
  If the property is sold or refinanced, the fees for releasing the mortgage (registration and bank handling fees) are deductible in that particular year.

- **Accounting fees**
  These may be deducted in the section relating to property deductions or elsewhere on your tax return.

- **Business deductions**
  It is also worth noting that when you own investment property, you are effectively operating a business. There is a separate list of deductions that does not directly relate to your property but to your business. These claims may form part of your property deductions or may constitute a separate section on business deductions. Such a list might include: property investment manuals; investment magazines; newspapers; seminars; depreciation on equipment (books, wheelbarrow, computer); costs associated with a home-office or place of business, car, and many of the costs already listed as property deductions but for which it is difficult to proportion to each property directly (e.g. mower fuel – how much did you use where?). Note that there is a subtle difference between a home-office and a place of business. Home-office costs may include telephone, lighting and depreciation but if it is called your "place of business" (a particular place set aside for business only), then additional claims of rates, insurance, repairs and interest may be claimed as a percentage of the floor area.

Special proportional deductions

There are many instances where a property may be partly used for other purposes. In these cases, there is a proportional claim for deductions. Examples of where this may occur include:

- **Joint owners**
  Deductions may be proportionately shared between joint owners (usually 50% unless specified otherwise in a document).

- **Boarders**
  If you are a single person and share your home with two boarders who each have full access to all parts of the property, then you can claim two-thirds of all property expenses.

- **Holiday homes**
  If you have a holiday home, you can claim a proportion of expenses for the period that the house was actually let *and* available for letting (i.e. when the agent was actively seeking tenants as opposed to when you were simply not using it).

4.2 Negative gearing

Borrowing money for property investment is called gearing (or leverage) and can significantly increase the returns on investment. Negative gearing simply means that the rent is not sufficient to cover the interest payments plus expenses. Current legislation enables you to claim this loss against income from other sources provided that it was your intention to eventually earn income from the particular property. The tax benefits from this may be so high that you need contribute very little to the cash flow of your investment property. Negative gearing means that the taxman is contributing to your property investment and it is simply a form of subsidised housing. In many cases, it is cheaper for the Government to pay you to house the needy than to provide Housing Corporation accommodation. *To gain the maximum benefit from negative gearing, the property should be in the name of the highest income earner.*

The current tax scales are:

Income	Rate
Below $34,200	21.5%
Above $34,200	33%

If you earn more than $34,200, you will be paying tax on your "top" dollar at 33%. Consequently, all tax deductions that you can make will be "saving" tax at the same rate i.e. 33%. Even at incomes below $34,200, tax deductions will save you 21.5%.

The following two examples show you exactly how negative gearing works.

Example 1

Assume a house costs $100,000 and is bought with a loan of $101,989 (additional funds to cover purchasing and borrowing costs). Rent is $150/week ($7,800/year) and as given in the example in Section 4.1, total deductions are $19,790. Assume also that earned income is $45,000.

Normal earned income	=	$45,000.00
Normal tax	=	$12,071.25

After house purchase

Rent	=	$7,800	
Total income	=	$52,800	($7,800 + 45,000)
Deductions	=	$19,790	
Taxable income	=	$33,010	($52,800 − 19,790)
New tax	=	$8,114.55	
Tax saving	=	$3,956.70	($12,071.25 − 8,114.55)

Note that if the actual costs were only $15,361 (as outlined in Section 4.1), then the real cost to you is $3,604.30 (i.e. $7,800 − 15,361 + 3,956.70). But the capital gain if calculated as 10% of the valued $100,000) of the property, is $10,000.

Example 2

If the same house is bought with the same conditions as above except that the income of the purchaser is $30,000, then the outcome would be as follows:

Normal earned income	=	$30,000
Normal tax	=	$7,200

After house purchase

Rent	=	$7,800	
Total income	=	$37,800	($30,000 + 7,800)
Deductions	=	$19,790	
Taxable income	=	$18,010	($37,800 − 19,790)
New tax	=	$4,322	
Tax saving	=	$2,878	($7,200 − 4,322)

From the above two examples, you can see that "negative gearing" applied to property investments favours the higher income earner. This is certainly not an indication that lower income earners should not invest in property, but simply that the tax benefits are not as great. As demonstrated later (Section 5), the after-tax return on investment for lower income levels may still be far better than any other form of investment.

Bear in mind that since your PAYE deductions are based solely on your salaried income, the tax benefits of being negatively geared may not accrue until your tax account is settled, which may be up to 24 months after a negative cash flow. If your property or properties are negatively geared to the extent that the loss totally cancels your salaried income, then you may apply to the Inland Revenue Department for a special tax code, which, if approved, reduces your regular PAYE deductions accordingly. However, this ruling will not apply to many investors.

4.3 Goods and Services Tax (GST)

The GST implications for residential property investors are very minor. Unlike commercial leases, which attract GST, residential rentals are exempt from GST. Since the final goods or services offered for sale (in our case rental accommodation) do not attract GST, then it follows that the GST-component of expenses incurred (such as tradesmen and hardware for repairs) cannot be claimed from or reimbursed by the GST department. Instead, the entire amount inclusive of GST may be deducted as an expense. Consequently, there is little benefit to be had from being GST-registered, and accordingly many residential property investors do not bother.

Similarly, the purchase and sale of residential real estate is exempt from GST, so that once again there are no benefits to be had from being GST-registered. Note, however, that if you buy residential properties not with the aim of renting them, but with the aim of selling them at a profit (i.e. trading in properties) then you become liable for GST on the sale of the properties and you may claim the GST on purchase. In this case, you may also claim the GST-component of incidental expenses.

Section 5. Computer Analysis of Rate of Return

We will show you how the rate of return on investment property can be in excess of 50% *after-tax*. To do this, we have developed a computer program available using the order form at the back of this book which produces a spreadsheet (shown below) giving the projected capital growth, cash flow and real rate of return for an investment property. In simple terms, it is as if your investment property is a bank in which you continually deposit money; you receive interest on all the deposits such that, at the end, the total amount you have is the equity you have built up in the property. The effective rate of interest that you would have received is actually the after-tax Internal Rate of Return or IRR. This combines the capital growth, yield, return on deposit, return on all cash outlays *and* tax advantages to produce an after-tax rate of return on the cash flow. The spreadsheet below contains details for an investment property purchased for $100,000 with $510 in purchase costs. No deposit was necessary, and loan costs amounted to $1,479. The loan was thus $101,989.

de Roos Associates

Assumptions and initial inputs		yr 1	yr 2	yr 3	yr 4	yr 5
1 Property value($)	$100,000	106,000	112,360	119,102	126,248	133,823
2 Purchase costs ($)	$510					
3 Deposit ($)	0					
4 Loan ($)	$101,989					
5 Equity ($)	–$1,989	4,011	10,371	17,113	24,259	**31,834**
6 Capital Growth rate	6%					
7 Inflation rate	5%					
8 Gross rent ($/wk, $/yr)	$165	8,408	8,829	9,270	9.734	10,220
9 **Cash deductions**						
10 Interest on loan ($)	12%	12,239	12,239	12,239	12,239	12,239
11 Expenses ($)	13%	1,115	1,171	1,230	1,291	1,356
12 *Pre-tax cash flow*	0	– 4,946	– 4,581	– 4,198	– 3,796	– 3,374
13 **Non-cash deductions**						
14 Depreciation-building ($)	4%	2,800	2,688	2,580	2,477	2,378
15 Depreciation-chattels ($)	6,000	1,200	960	768	614	492
16 Loan costs ($)	1,479	1,479				
17 **Total deductions** ($)		18,833	17,057	16,816	16,621	16,464
18 Tax credit ($)	33%	3,440	2,715	2,490	2,273	2,060
19 *After-tax cash flow* ($)	0	–1,505	–1,865	–1,707	–1,523	–1,313
20 **Rate of return (IRR)**	57.84%	per year – and this is AFTER tax				
21 Before-tax equivalent	86.33%	Does your bank give you this rate?				

Notes on the spreadsheet items

1. House value

This represents the price paid for the property and is assumed to increase each year at a constant compound rate of growth (see Note 6).

2. Purchase costs

These include stamp duty (commercial property only) and your solicitor's fees. Solicitor's fees may vary from nothing (if you do it yourself) to about $900. In this case stamp duty is zero and solicitor's fees are assumed to be $510.

3. Deposit

This represents the total amount of cash that you wish to invest in the property. It not only represents the amount that you will pay towards the actual purchase price but also the various costs associated with purchase and borrowing. In the case above, it is assumed that there is no deposit and that the borrowings cover both the purchase price and all associated purchase and loan costs.

4. Loan

This is simply the total of all costs (house price, purchase costs, loan costs) less the amount of the deposit. In the above case, as the deposit is nothing, the loan represents the total of all costs.

5. Equity

This is the difference between the house value and the loan. The equity increases in line with the increasing value of the house because the loan is assumed to remain constant. (A principal plus interest loan may also be selected, in which case the amount of the loan outstanding diminishes over time.) In the example, the equity has reached $31,834 by the end of five years. Selling costs have not been deducted because the assumption is that the property is to be kept long-term and this spreadsheet represents an analysis over only part of that term.

6. Capital growth

This is the expected annual compound rate of increase of the property (assumed to be a conservative 6% in the example, even though it has averaged around 10% for the last 100 years).

7. Inflation rate

This is the expected inflation rate (5% per year in the example) and in this model affects the growth in rental, rates, insurance and maintenance.

8. Gross rent (/week and /year)

The first cell contains the expected weekly rent, while the rest of the row represents the corresponding annual rent calculated simply as the weekly rent times 52, and then diminished by the vacancy factor (2% in the example). It is assumed that the rent increases each year in line with inflation.

9. Cash deductions

These differ from "non-cash deductions" in that they are real cash outflows. There are two types of cash deductions – interest and rental expenses.

10. Interest on loan

The first cell represents the interest rate while the rest of the row represents the corresponding annual interest payments. The loan is assumed to be fixed-rate interest-only, but a Principal and Interest loan may also be selected.

11. Expenses

All real costs excluding the interest on the loan (see Section 4). In the example, this has been simply calculated as a fixed percentage (13%) of the annual rent. We consider 13% to be a reasonable guide to the expenses for a fairly new house with minimum maintenance that is self-managed. If professionally-managed, it would be about 23% and a typical breakdown might be:

Rates, insurance	10%
Agents commission	10%
Repairs, maintenance, car	3%
Total	23%

12. Before-tax cash flow

This is what flows in or out of your pocket before tax is taken into account. It is calculated as the gross rent less interest and expenses.

13. Non-cash deductions

The three types of tax deductions that indirectly affect your cash flow in the form of tax benefits are depreciation on the building, depreciation on chattels and loan costs.

14. Depreciation on building

See Section 4.1. This is the depreciation on the capital improvements value.

15. Depreciation on chattels

In this example the value of the chattels was approximated at 6% of the house value and the depreciation was claimed at 20%. Items and their depreciation rates are listed in Section 4.1.

16. Loan costs

These include various items associated with financing the purchase. The cost of individual items will vary between financial institutions. In the example, we have used the following costs:

Establishment fee (1% of loan)	1,020
Valuation fees	300
Registration of mortgage (x 2)	92
Registration of title	46
Search fees	21
	1,479

17. **Total deductions**

This is the sum of all deductions you can claim – both cash and non-cash.

18. **Tax credit**

The first cell represents the marginal tax rate (33% in this example). The rest of the row represents the annual tax credit or liability (i.e. the tax on the difference between rental income and total deductions). In this example, it is the annual tax refund.

19. **After-tax cash flow**

This is the amount of cash actually invested in the property each year.

20. **IRR**

The after-tax Internal Rate of Return on all monies invested over the period of time considered.

21. **Before-tax equivalent**

This is the interest rate that you bank would have to pay for you to get an equivalent rate of return.

Note that although the Internal Rate of Return is calculated over a period of five years to facilitate presentation of the whole spreadsheet, it is most desirable that the property be considered as a longer-term investment. In fact, the rate of return on this property will actually decline over time because increases in rent will gradually reduce the tax benefit to such an extent that instead of receiving a tax refund, you will be paying tax on rent. Before this situation is reached, the strategy would be to borrow additional funds to acquire more property and hence maintain the overall tax status.

Internal Rate of Return

The internal rate of return is now the generally accepted method of calculating the returns on cash flows with the time factor taken into account. Many books are available on the subject but in simple terms it can be described as follows. Consider that the money that you are outlaying for your investment property is being deposited in the bank each year and that interest is also added each year. At the end of a period of time, your bank account will register all your cash deposits plus interest and will be shown as a sum total of money. In the property investment example we have used, less than $2000 of after-tax cash flow (row 19 of the spreadsheet) is being injected into your property each year, interest is added each year (at the internal rate of 57.84%) and the sum total of what you have built up over five years is $31,834 (equity). If you were to deposit the same amounts into your bank account with an interest rate of 6% (9% before tax), you would have accrued only $9,505.

To achieve the same equity from these cash flows, a bank would have to offer 57.84% interest after tax (or 86.33% before tax).

Sensitivity analysis

As it is important to understand the effect of changes in the various inputs on the rate of return, the computer program has been designed to allow all of these inputs to be varied, with the resultant IRR calculated automatically. As an example of the sensitivity of the IRR to changes in the various inputs, the results obtained by changing one or more of the inputs are given below:

Change to Inputs	Internal Rate of Return (IRR)
	%
1. No change	57.84
2. Tax bracket = 21.5%	36.91
3. Expenses = 23%	43.41
4. Deposit = $5,000	34.69
5. Deposit = $10,000	27.24
6. Deposit = $20,000	20.70
7. Capital Growth = 10%	87.83

Calculating how much you need

As stated earlier in the book (Section 1), it may take as little as $80 per week to enter the property investment market. How much you need is determined by many factors such as house price, deposit, rent, interest rate, expenses, and marginal tax rate. The spreadsheet is a useful tool in calculating just how much you need for any given set of conditions. In the example given, approximately $1800 per year of after-tax cash flow can be translated in costing you just $36 per week. How much you need is dependent on your marginal tax rate. The program will calculate the weekly cash flow required for a property, and the number of similar properties which may safely be acquired.

Computer Program

Copies of the program used in the analysis of the above examples are available from de Roos Associates, P.O. Box 14, Christchurch (see order form at the back of this book).

Section 6.
Property Management

Rental property can either be managed by the owner or a professional property management company (usually a real estate firm). Management fees vary but, as a guide, they are typically 7.5% plus a letting fee equivalent to one or two week's rent. The total is usually about 10% of the gross rent.

Choosing a property manager

A good professional property manager can be well worthwhile if you don't want the hassles associated with tenants. Never forget that tenants are a crucial part of your investment. The wonderful thing about property investment is that you can do as little or as much as you like. If you have the right business approach while still remaining sympathetic to tenants needs, then you may like to manage the property yourself. If you let the rent remain at $100 for six years because you've become too friendly with the tenants, then a property manager is definitely for you. If you like fixing taps, painting fences, landscaping gardens, etc., then do it, regardless of whether you have a property manager or not. Otherwise get a tradesman or get your property manager to organise one for you.

If you decide to use a manager instead of doing it yourself, you must take the trouble of finding a "good one". That means finding a real estate agent who runs his rent roll as a business and not just as a necessary conjunct to his selling business. Using a manager does not mean that you lose control. You can still do as much or as little as you wish — i.e. specify the type of tenant, negotiate the rent, paint the house, etc. In many cases, the property manager simply acts as a buffer so that you do not fall into the trap of becoming so friendly with your tenants that you are reluctant to maintain the rent at market levels (just because your neighbour is your milkman does not mean that you get milk half price). Never lose sight of the fact that property investment is a business and for it to be successful, it must operate along proper business lines. Regardless of whether or not you are managing the property yourself, the following points should be considered:

- **Tenant screening**
  Contrary to popular belief, people with young children and pets often make good tenants. Simply state in the lease that pets are to be kept outside at all times. Rather than trying to choose tenants on the basis of such things as their marital status,

it is far more important to select them on the basis of their ability to pay and cleanliness. A reference from a previous landlord or employer together with a quick look at a prospective tenant's last place of residence may be all that is required.

- **Maintenance**
Remember that it is your superannuation fund that you are running – don't let it and your property become run down. Tenants dislike miserly landlords – especially those who collect the rent in a Porsche yet refuse to fix a leaking roof. A property kept in a good condition attracts good tenants whereas grotty houses attract grotty tenants. All your repair bills are tax deductible so the taxman is helping you pay for your repairs anyway. In addition, well maintained properties are always much easier to rent, which can be especially important at times when vacancies are high.

- **Rent**
Rent *must* be maintained at or close to the prevailing market rate. However, if there is a temporary over-supply of rental accommodation, a slightly lower rent may mean fewer vacancies and should attract a larger number of tenants from which you can choose. But if you fall into the trap of increasing the rent only once the tenants have left, you may eventually find that the tenants are on such a good thing that they cannot afford to leave, so you never get the chance to increase the rent.

- **Relationship with tenants**
Good property management is often about good people management. Even if you use a property manager, it is good to take an interest in and get to know the tenants. It is surprising how people respond to a little attention but always try and maintain the relationship as one of professional courtesy. You do not want to become so friendly that you find it impossible to maintain the rent at market levels.

- **Preparing tenancy agreements**
A tenancy agreement protects both you and the tenant. Longer term agreements (up to 12 months) are becoming more popular, and additional clauses can be added if you wish. It is a good idea to include carpet cleaning and pest control as part of the tenants responsibility.

- **Handling arrears**
Prevention is better than cure – good tenant selection is critical. Having a good but firm relationship with the tenant may also solve any problems before it leads to court action which may prove costly to you and still may recoup no rent (if they don't have it, they can't pay it).

- **Advertising**
Property managers may not have to advertise as they have a lot of "walk in" enquiries. If you are managing the property yourself, placing an advertisement in the local newspaper will usually get a good response.

- **Vacancies**

  These must be kept to a minimum. An acceptable vacancy factor is about 4%. This means that at any point in time, 4% of rentable houses are vacant or that for 4% of the year (i.e. two weeks), a property will be vacant. In many cases, well maintained properties in reasonable locations and listed at market rent should have no vacancies at all.

- **Bond**

  This can be the equivalent of up to four weeks rent and must be held with the Bond Centre at the Ministry of Housing.

- **Payment system**

  A property manager will collect the rent and will either mail you a monthly cheque or deposit it in a bank account of your choice. If you are managing it yourself, you may wish to visit the tenant every fortnight to collect the rent, or alternatively have the rent transferred into your bank account by automatic payments.

- **Inspection**

  These should be at least six-monthly but it certainly doesn't hurt to drive past your property more frequently.

- **Assistance**

  Your local Property Investors Association can assist you with most aspects of property management, including the selection of tradesmen, tenancy agreements and advice on how to handle rent arrears.

Section 7. The A to Z of What If

- **Capital growth is not 10%?**
  Although there are no guarantees, for centuries property has been a secure means of building wealth. Average annual compound growth has been 10% over the last 900 years in Britain, 12% over the last 100 years in Australia, and 10% over the last 100 years in New Zealand. There appears to be no reason for these rates of growth not to continue.

- **But I'm afraid of borrowing large sums of money!**
  The golden rule of borrowing money is to borrow for appreciating assets (e.g. property), not for consumables or things that depreciate in value. The debt is a *controlled* debt and correct management should ensure peace of mind (see Section 3.2).

- **The mortgage company goes bust**
  You have their money so you cannot lose it in the same way as if the company has yours. It may simply be a matter of another financial institution taking over the mortgage company or you may have the slight inconvenience and expense of refinancing elsewhere.

- **I can't afford the initial cash flow deficit**
  Borrow 5% more than you need – there is nothing like money in the bank to help you sleep.

- **Interest rates rise**
  If you are at all concerned about interest rates rising, choose to borrow where rates are fixed for a minimum of three years at a time.

- **You need money urgently**
  Don't sell. Rather it is preferable to:
  – use your credit cards;
  – take out a personal loan;
  – take our a second mortgage.

- **The house burns down**
  Make sure that you are adequately insured and this means taking out sufficient cover which will:
  - replace the building;
  - reimburse the lost rent;
  - pay the demolition and architect's fees;
  - meet any public liability costs (you don't need someone suing you for $300,000 because they burnt their fingers).

- **The bread winner meets with misfortune**
  Take out sufficient life and disability insurance and have sufficient cash reserves until alternative arrangements can be made.

- **Divorce is a possibility**
  Consult your solicitor first to have a written statement as to the equitable division of assets, regardless of title of ownership.

- **There is a severe depression**
  Keep sufficient funds in reserve. Successful investors are those able to hold long term to reap the rewards of future recovery.

- **My accountant doesn't like the idea**
  Accountants are specialists in their area of expertise – accounting. They will expertly complete the tax forms for you after you have provided them with all the figures. They are NOT specialists in property investment and should never be relied on as such.

- **Vacancy factors are high**
  Supply and demand in rental properties is cyclic. If there is a period of time when there are many properties for rent, the following points should be considered:
  - good professional property managers are experts in obtaining tenants over slow times. They help minimise vacancies;
  - rents may need to be lowered marginally to attract tenants;
  - well-located properties rent more easily than those out in the middle of nowhere, so be careful where you buy in the first place;
  - well-maintained properties rent more easily.

- **Tenants get behind in rent**
  With a good manager, this should not happen. Taking care to select good tenants in the first place is the best solution.

- **Maintenance is a problem**
A good house attracts good tenants who will look after it. If problems occur, the agent has access to the required maintenance people. Make sure that you pay attention to maintenance problems immediately.

- **Real estate prices stagnate**
Holding on to the house for at least 10 years ensures a buffer against any cycles in the market.

- **There is an over-supply of houses for sale or to rent**
The cyclical nature of real estate usually means that within a short period, there will be a corresponding under-supply of houses available. Long-term investment lessens the time impact of market cycles.

- **I have no deposit for an investment house**
Use the equity in your own home. Cash is not necessary as a deposit. Having sufficient assets against which to borrow is all that is required.

- **I don't like real estate**
Real estate is only the vehicle for the high rate of return — a means to an end and not the end itself.

- **What about a holiday home?**
Be careful to distinguish between an investment property and a luxury. For an investment property, you should be using the unit when it is not let rather than letting it when you are not using it. By the time you have created your investment portfolio, you should be able to afford a luxurious holiday unit that you can use any time you desire.

- **You don't have the time to look after the property**
A good property manager is the key. He/she will do most things from paying the rates to arranging for the shower to be fixed.

- **You wish to buy a house in partnership with a friend**
This is one sure recipe to lose a friend. If the investment is worthwhile, do it yourself. Different people will have different ideas on investments. However, if it is the only way that you can afford to get started in property investment, then have a go but beware of the pitfalls.

- **The tax laws change**
The Government is unlikely to abolish the negative gearing laws because of the impact on those who pay rent. In the unlikely event that it does, the change should not be retrospective. But, even without negative gearing, your return should still be better than other forms of investment, and your debt should be adjusted to balance the rental income.

- **Capital gains tax may be introduced**

  Unless a Capital Gains Tax is levied on unrealised capital gains, if you don't sell, you don't pay. Furthermore, because it would apply only to that gain over and above the rate of inflation, it is usually only minimal if you do sell in the long term.

- **Rents do not increase**

  Rents increase in cycles similar to house prices. Over a 10 year period, the rent should move with inflation.

- **You miss out on the investment of a lifetime**

  It's our opinion that the "once in a lifetime" investment opportunity comes along about once a month.

- **I don't understand the basis of real estate investment**

  Knowledge minimises risks and mistakes, and maximises returns. Be prepared to learn from mistakes (both your own and those of others) and seek professional advice.

Section 8. Reading List

Successful property investors usually have three basic characteristics:

- They have sound financial principles
- They are highly motivated to succeed
- They divert their energies, knowledge, and money into property investment.

With this in mind, the list of recommended reading outlined below has been separated into these categories.

8.1 Financial Principles

- **"Making Money Made Simple"**
  by Noel Whittaker and Roger Moses (Beckett Publishers) 1992
  Highly recommended. The basic principles of handling money explained in very simple terms. Completely revised – a must for everyone.

- **"Making More Money"**
  by Noel Whittaker and Roger Moses (Beckett Publishers) 1991

- **"Unlimited Success in Personal Investments"**
  by Don Stammer (Wrightbooks) 1989
  A good summary of the options available. It is not particularly detailed, but makes good light reading.

8.2 Motivation to Succeed

- **"Think and Grow Rich"**
  by Napoleon Hill (Wilshire Book Company) 1966. (First published in 1937)
  A highly motivating book written over 50 years ago in a very simple and easy to read style. Still very relevant today.

- **"The Greatest Success in the World"** and **"The University of Success"**
  by Og Mandino (Bantam Books) 1981
  Og Mandino's books are very short and his classic story-telling method is inspirational in identifying the principles of success.

- **"Power to Choose"**
  by Hayden Sargent (Boolarong Publications) 1989
  A wonderful book, very simply written and suitable for all ages. It deals with self-motivation and success and will give you loads of self-confidence.

8.3 Property Investment

- **"Riches from Real Estate"**
  by Fred Johnson and Brendan Whiting (Fredan Pty Ltd) 1979
  A must for all. A well written, easy to follow book, which espouses the simple but effective philosophy of "buy and never sell". If you read nothing else, read this! Other books by the same authors are:
  "How to Get Real Estate Rich"
  "More Riches from Real Estate"
  "New Ways to Real Estate Wealth"
  "New Ways to Real Estate Wealth in New Zealand"
  "The Way Ahead to Property Wealth"

- **"Unlimited Success in Real Estate"**
  by Christopher Lang (Brooks Waterloo Publishers) 1986
  A very light reading book. Lots of good ideas, together with the author's own personal experiences. The emphasis is on creative thinking.

- **"Unlimited Success in Property Development"**
  by Christopher Lang (Brooks Waterloo Publishers) 1989
  Short and sweet but with some innovative ideas in investing. Worthwhile reading if only for the lateral thoughts.

- **"How to use your HOME EQUITY to invest in a second house – and a third"**
  by Lois Towart (Book Works Pty Ltd) 1989
  A very good book if you're starting out but only superficially touches on such important topics as finance and tax. It gets bogged down in trivia relating to all properties – not just investment property.

- **"Creating Wealth"** *
  by Robert G. Allen (Simon and Schuster) 1983
  An American book which again promotes the idea of accumulating residential property as a life-long investment. Another book by the same author: **"Nothing Down"** (Simon and Schuster), is nowhere near as good. It is based on acquiring apartment blocks in the USA with no cash deposit and is somewhat repetitive.

- **"How to Make it When You're Cash Poor"** *
  by Hollis Norton (Simon and Schuster) 1985
  Very similar to the Robert Allen books. Emphasis is on the creative methods of purchasing houses with no cash deposits.

- **"Jones on Property"**
  by Bob Jones (Fourth Estate Books) 1977
  Out of print now but well worth reading.

- **"Estate Magazine"**
  A property periodical with topical information and discussions. Obtainable through your local Property Investors Association as part of their membership fee.
  (For details of your local group write to NZPIF, P.O. Box 4396, Christchurch. Telephone (03) 366-5978.)

- **"The New Zealand Landlord"**
  A monthly magazine with articles, commentary, and statistics (updated for each issue) on residential property trends in New Zealand.
  (For details telephone (09) 815-8644 or fax (09) 815-8643.)

* **Note** that American books on property investment are worth reading for their creative ideas on financing and motivational techniques, but readers should be aware that American property transactions are somewhat different from those in New Zealand. In New Zealand, few sales involves vendor finance, whereas in America, almost 90% of sales involve vendor finance, of which a good proportion including assumable mortgages (i.e. the house is sold complete with the mortgage which does not have to be re-negotiated with the bank). As a result, most American books on the subject are all about creatively manipulating the purchase of the mortgage, not the house!

Some of the books listed above are now out of print, but may be found in libraries or secondhand bookshops.

Property Investment Analysis
• software for property investors

PIA is a high performance computer program that provides an instant analysis of investment properties as an aid to acquisition decisions.

PIA calculates capital value, equity build-up, pre-tax cash flows, after tax returns, and the Internal Rate of Return (IRR) for up to 40 years ahead. Useful printouts enable investors to make wise investment decisions, while real estate agents can enhance and streamline their listings by including pertinent information for clients. Bank managers find the printouts invaluable in mortgage advance decision-making.

The program takes account of:
– depreciation (on both buildings and chattels)
– Solicitors' fees
– stamp duty (where applicable)
– mortgage interest payments
– mortgage structure (Interest Only or Principal plus Interest)
– loan application fees
– inflation rate
– capital growth rate
– investor's marginal tax rate
– negative gearing

Features:
– extremely simple to operate
– single screen full-colour spreadsheet layout
– full help facilities on screen, with prompts for input variables
– pre-selected values (defaults) for stamp duty rate, taxation rates, depreciation schedules, and loan acquisition fees
– instant sensitivity analysis to show effects of changes to any variable such as interest rates and rental levels
– prints two six-page reports including spreadsheets, tables and graphs
– calculates the tax benefits of an investment
– determines an investor's borrowing capacity
– PC and Mac versions available
– comes complete with a copy of the book "The New Zealand Investor's Guide to Making Money in Residential Real Estate" and "Building Wealth through Investment Property" by Jan Somers and Dolf de Roos
– total cost is $595 plus GST

de Roos Associates Ltd
ORDER FORM

Name: _____

Address: _____

_____

Telephone: _____

Please: ☐ put me on or ☐ keep me on or ☐ remove me from your mailing list

☐ note my **new** address above (the old address was: _____)

(If a friend or relative wants to be added to our mailing list, simply send us their details)

MAKING MONEY

The New Zealand Investor's Guide to Making Money in Residential Real Estate by Dolf de Roos and Jan Somers: ____ copies @ $25 each inc GST: $_____

Building Wealth in Changing Times by Jan Somers (written for Australia but much of the material is relevant to NZ): ____ copies @ $29 each inc GST: $_____

Building Wealth through Investment Property by Dolf de Roos and Jan Somers: ____ copies @ $29 each inc GST: $_____

BUILDING WEALTH in *Changing Times* Jan Somers

PIA
Property Investment Analysis software: $595 + GST = $669.37: $_____
(includes any 3 books from the list above - please specify)

PICS
Property Investment Computer Slideshow: $595 + GST = $669.37: $_____
(includes any 10 books from the list above - please specify)

BUILDING WEALTH Through Investment Property

Name to appear in either program:_____

Please specify ☑ either ☐ PC or ☐ MAC software

Postage, packaging and handling inc GST: $ **2.50**

TOTAL AMOUNT PAYABLE (inc GST): $_____

Payment: Ref: MM

☐ Cheque (enclosed)

☐ VISA   Cardholder's Name: _____

☐ Mastercard   Card Number: _____

☐ Diners Club   Expiry Date: _____

☐ American Express   Cardholder's Signature   _____

Please post to: de Roos Associates
                         PO Box 14
                         Christchurch

NOTES